Gutsy Girls

Strong, Christian Women Who Impacted the World

Book Three:
Fanny Crosby

Amy L. Sullivan

Illustrated by Beverly Ann Wines

This Book Belongs To:

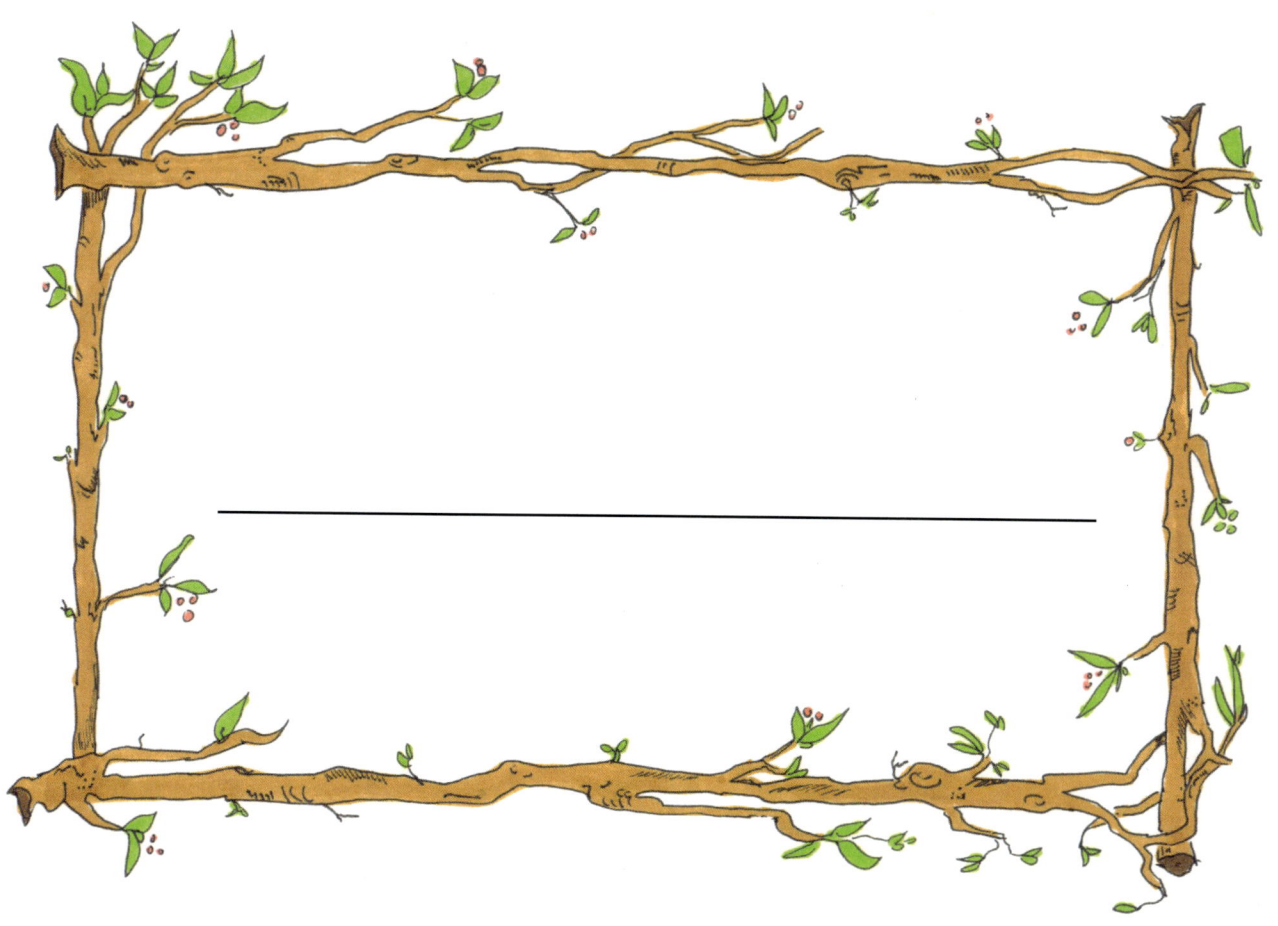

Gutsy Girl

gutsy \guht-see\ adjective: brave, courageous, daring.

Showing determination even when your heart beats fast, your hands grow sweaty, and you fear failure.

Dedications

To the girl who first called me Mom, my Amelia. —A.L.S.

To my heroes, my parents, you are my angels on earth. Dad, I will always persevere. Mom, I will always dance. I love you! —B.A.W.

Gutsy Girls: *Strong Christian Women Who Impacted the World*
Book Three: *Fanny Crosby*

All Rights Reserved © 2016 Amy L. Sullivan

Illustrations © 2016 Beverly A. Wines

No part of this book may be reproduced, scanned, or distributed in any printed or electronic form without the express written permission of the publisher except for the use of brief quotations in a book review.

ISBN-13: 978-1539557449

ISBN-10: 1539557448

Printed in the United States of America

Gutsy Girls

Strong, Christian Women Who Impacted the World

Book Three:
Fanny Crosby

Amy L. Sullivan

Illustrated by Beverly Ann Wines

Francis Jane Crosby was like most babies. She cooed, cried, and liked to clap. And like most parents, Francis' mother and father decided their child needed a nickname.

"I know! Let's call her Fanny!"

"Fanny? Oh, yes! Fanny. I like the sound of that."

Although Fanny was similar to other babies, something made her different; baby Fanny was blind.

Some say Fanny became blind after contracting a terrible eye infection. Others say she lost her ability to see when a stranger pretending to be a doctor applied a wrap made of hot mustard seeds to her eyes.

Regardless, baby Fanny's world looked like a window covered in ice where only a small amount of color and a tiny bit of light sneaked through.

As Fanny grew, being blind didn't stop her from doing the same things as other children.

She could climb trees, play the guitar, frolic in fields, complete chores, make friends, ride a horse, sing in church, identify birds, and sew a shirt.

If you gave Fanny a leaf, she could easily tell what kind of tree it came from just by feeling and smelling it.

"Well, I know this leaf isn't from a maple, oak, or birch tree. I bet it fell from the wild apple tree!"

But since Fanny was blind, there was something she couldn't do in the same way as other children—learn.

Fanny tried to attend school.

"Fanny, this is the letter *A*. Can you say *A*?"

"Um, I can't see what you are holding, but I can recite the first four books of both the Old and New Testaments."

Fanny frustrated her teachers.

She was smart, but they didn't have time to figure out how to teach her. So most of the time, Fanny didn't go to school. Not going to school was a big, big problem because more than anything, Fanny wanted to learn.

One day, when Fanny was fifteen-years-old, her mother learned about the New York Institution for the Blind. It was a school created specifically for children who were blind.

Since Fanny was a little girl, she prayed that she would have a chance to learn, and Fanny knew that even though she would have to leave her family and live at the school, this was her chance.

Days at Fanny's new school were busy, and students followed a strict schedule:

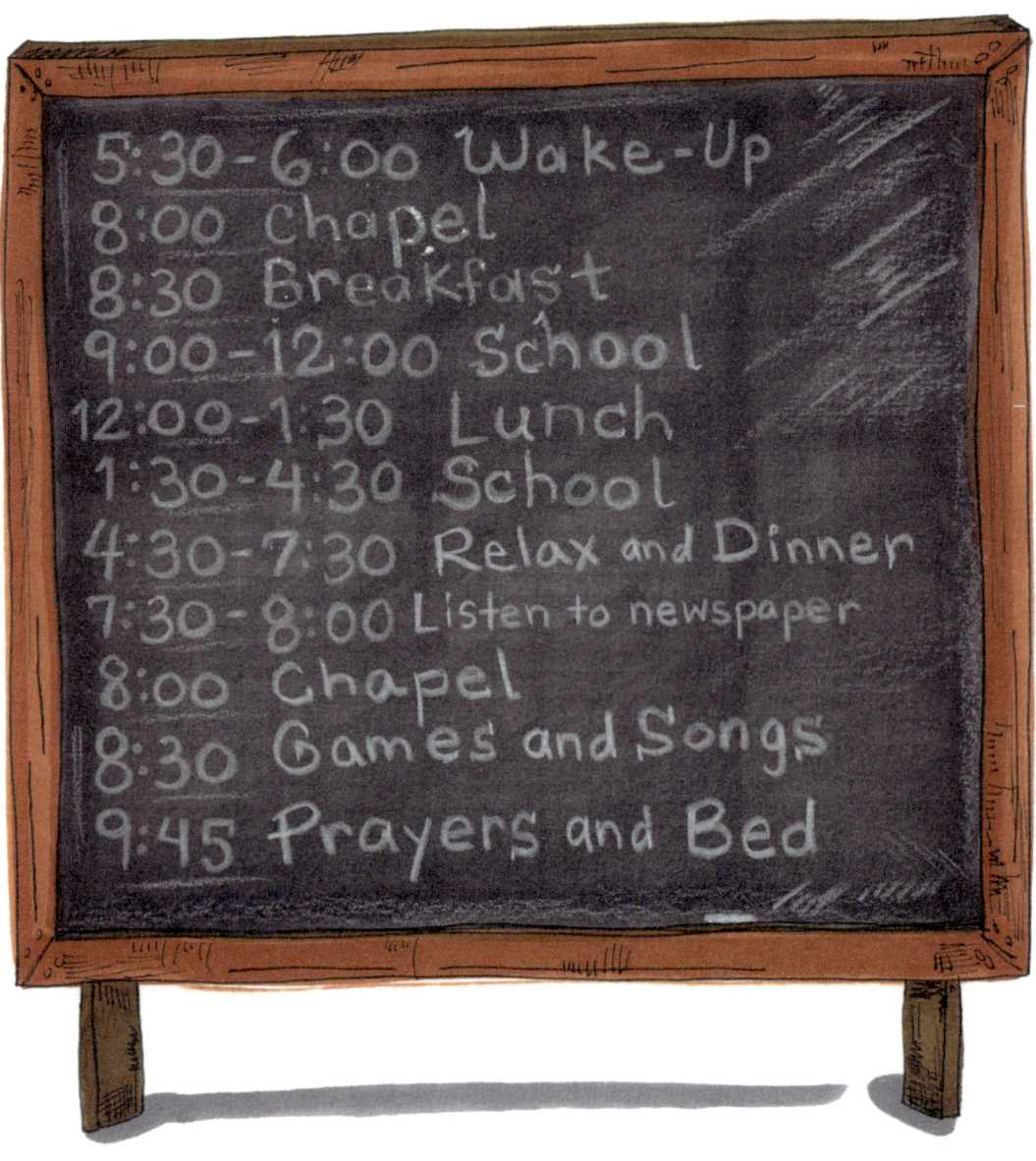

At school, Fanny learned in new ways.

Teachers taught geography by using maps with raised lines and grooves so students could feel the difference between land and water. Teachers taught reading by using embossed letters, which poked out from the page. Teachers taught math by giving students small, metal slates with holes to assist them with counting.

Fanny was like you and me. She excelled at some subjects in school and struggled with others.

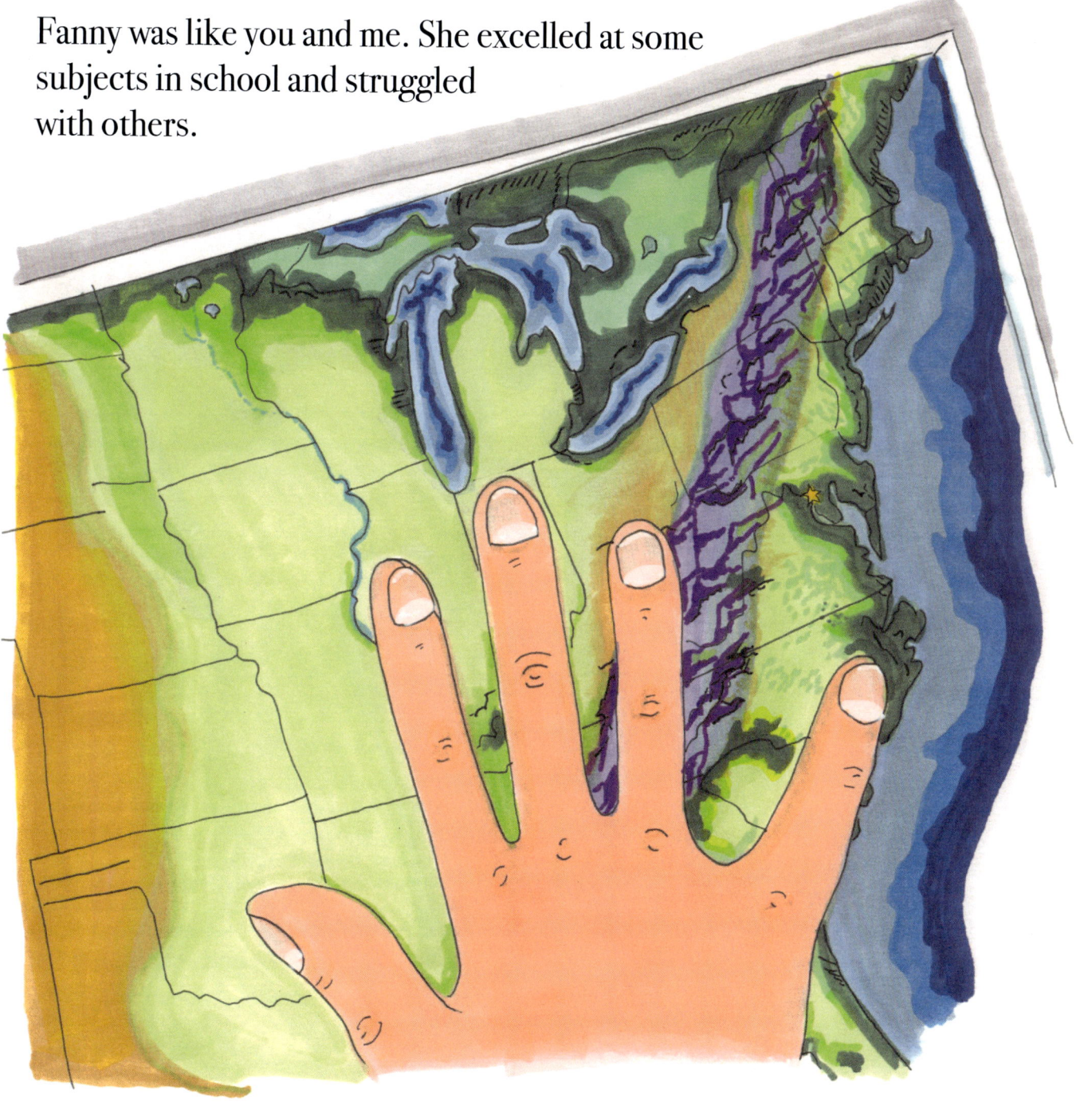

If someone read information to her just one time, Fanny could accurately remember it. Fanny could create stories and poems, and she could easily distinguish between voices. But Fanny did not like math. Numbers left her confused. Fanny called math . . .

The GreAt MoNSteR!

Fanny's handwriting was so poor that she struggled to even write her name.

"Fanny, your writing looks like a pile of spider legs!"

Eventually, Fanny gave up trying to write. Instead, she had friends write down her poems and thoughts.

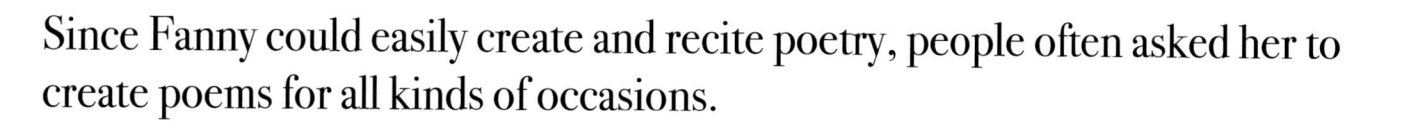

Since Fanny could easily create and recite poetry, people often asked her to create poems for all kinds of occasions.

When a teacher fell asleep and later awoke to find a mouse in his long hair, Fanny wrote a poem.

When important guests, politicians, scientists, and authors visited the school, Fanny wrote a poem.

When Fanny was asked to speak in front of Congress, Fanny wrote a poem.

Writing and reciting poetry allowed Fanny to meet many famous people, even presidents!

"It's nice to meet you, President John Quincy Adams."

"Dinner sounds lovely, President Van Buren."

"What a pleasure to shake your hand, President Tyler."

"I'd love to walk through campus with you, President Polk."

"What an honor, President Lincoln."

"Ah, yes, I think we will be lifelong friends, President Cleveland."

One day, Fanny was asked to write poetry for a hymn. Hymns are songs sung in some churches. Although Fanny worried she wouldn't be able to write the words to a song, she asked God to help her, and something amazing happened.

Fanny wrote hymn after hymn after hymn. Fanny wrote hymns quickly and easily. She composed hymns that became popular and were sung by people in churches everywhere. Fanny created so many hymns that she had to write under a fake name called a pseudonym.

"When people open hymnals in church, they will find a book full of songs written by Fanny Crosby!"

"We can't have that. Is there any way you can write the words to the hymns under another name, too?"

Fanny didn't want people thinking of her when they sang. She wanted people thinking of God. So when Fanny finished a hymn, instead of writing her name as the author, she created a made-up name. In fact, Fanny chose more than two hundred pseudonyms to write under.

Here are only a few of the names she used:

Annie L. James

Arthur J. Langdon

Cora Linden

Emily S. Prentiss

FLORA DAYTON

George Sampson

Grace J. Francis

Henrieatta Blair

James Apple

JULIA STERLING

Leah Carleton

Louise W. Tilden

Minnie B. Lowry

Miss Grace Elliot

Mrs. Fanny J. Van Alstyne

Mrs. Helen Wells

Mrs. Kate Smiling

Mrs. Leah Carleton

Mrs. Lizzie Wilson

MRS. ROSE MATTHEWS

MYRA JUDSON

Rian A. Dykes

Because writing hymns didn't take Fanny a long time, she decided to show God's love in other ways, too. Fanny packed her belongings and moved.

She could have moved somewhere fancy.

Fanny could have moved to a place where people would recognize her when she walked down the street and say, "Hey, isn't that the famous Fanny Crosby?"

But Fanny decided that was not what God wanted. God wanted Fanny to be with His people who felt forgotten.

God wanted Fanny to move into one of the largest tenements in New York City and become a part of the community.

Fanny embraced her life in the city. She loved entertaining people and meeting new friends, but that wasn't enough. Fanny volunteered and worked with people who were sick and

                    people who were homeless

                                  and people others worked to avoid.

As the years passed, Fanny's determination to serve God and others increased.

Fanny lectured.

"Let me tell you what God has done in my life."

And she wrote hymns.

Fanny served.

"Dear heart, you are loved and adored!"

And she wrote hymns.

Fanny played.

"Of course, I'd love a ride on your sled!"

And she wrote hymns.

Fanny was even adopted by the Eel Clan of the Onondaga Indian Tribe.

"I've always been concerned about American Indians.
I'd love to be a member of your tribe!"

And Fanny wrote hymns.

No one knows exactly how many hymns Fanny wrote, but experts estimate it was more than nine thousand!

The more Fanny wrote, the more her songs traveled across the nation and across the world reaching millions of people.

Even today, almost two hundred years after Fanny lived, Fanny's songs can be heard in churches and even on the radio.

Fanny Crosby showed the world what happens when a person uses her skills and talents to honor God. She refused to let any obstacle—including blindness—get in the way of God's plan for her life.

That's gutsy.

Words for Gutsy Girls

1. **Congress** - the legislative part of the United States government, which makes laws and consists of the Senate and the House of Representatives.

2. **coo** - a soft and gentle sound.

3. **distinguish** - to mark as different.

4. **embossed** - a raised surface.

5. **frolic** - to move around playfully.

6. **pseudonym** - a name someone uses instead of his or her real name.

7. **tenements** - overcrowded and often rundown buildings where multiple families live.

Sources

Blumhofer, Edith. *Her Heart Can See: The Life and Hymns of Fanny J. Crosby*. Grand Rapids, Michigan: Eerdmans Publishing Company, 2005.

DeRusha, Michelle. *50 Women Every Christian Should Know: Learning From Heroines of the Faith*. Grand Rapids, Michigan: Baker Books, 2014.

Ruffin, Bernard. *Fanny Crosby: The Hymn Writer*. Uhrichsville, Ohio: Barbour Publishing Incorporated, 1976.

Travis, Lucille. *Fanny Crosby: The Blind Girl's Song*. Scotland, United Kingdom: CF4Kids, 2013.

Historical Note on Fanny Crosby

Fanny Crosby was born in 1820 in the small village of Brewster, fifty miles north of New York City. Often questioned about the burden of her blindness, Fanny repeatedly told people she viewed being blind as a gift from God.

Two of Fanny's most popular hymns, "Safe in the Arms of Jesus" and "Blessed Assurance," are still sung in churches today. In addition to writing lyrics, Fanny also wrote two autobiographies and thousands of poems.

Even though Fanny was known for being a gifted hymn writer, she spent much of her time serving others. Fanny created pills to help fight cholera, insisted on living in one of the city's worst tenements, gave away almost everything she earned, knitted mittens for soldiers, counseled prisoners, and constantly spoke of God's great love.

Fanny died at the age of 94 in 1915.

Fun Facts About Fanny Crosby

Favorite flower: violet.

Favorite items to carry: a tiny Bible and a small silk American flag.

Amount of money Fanny earned for the hymns she wrote: typically between $1.00-$2.00/hymn.

Fanny's favorite time to write hymns: after midnight.

Other hobbies: Fanny enjoyed playing pranks. As a child, she hid the postman's pen and pad. She even stole a watermelon from the school's garden.

Gutsy Girls:
Strong Christian Women Who Impacted the World

Book One: Gladys Aylward

Book Two: Sisters, Corrie and Betsie ten Boom

Book Three: Fanny Crosby

Book Four: Jennifer Wiseman

Book Five: Ruby Bridges (Coming February, 2017)

For free educational materials for classrooms, churches, and families, visit the author's website, AmyLSullivan.com.

About the Author

Amy L. Sullivan doesn't always feel brave, but her picture book series, *Gutsy Girls: Strong Christian Women Who Impacted the World,* allows her to comb through history and steal wisdom from the great women who came before her. Amy lives with her handsome husband, two daughters, naughty dog, and lazy cat in the mountains of Western North Carolina. Connect with Amy at AmyLSullivan.com.

About the Illustrator

Beverly Ann Wines is an illustrator, painter, and art teacher. Beverly's art reflects who she is and what she loves. Beverly's art can be found in bookstores, homes, and galleries across the nation. You can learn more about Beverly's work by emailing her at Bvrlywines@aol.com or visiting her website beverlysartandsoul.weebly.com.

Made in the USA
Lexington, KY
16 March 2018